You're Nearly There

Christian Sex Education for Preteens

Revised Edition

Mary Kehle

Harold Shaw Publishers
Wheaton, Illinois   89175

Cover photo: David Singer

Inside photos: Richard Ball, p. 44; Tim Botts, p. 56; David Maas, p. 50; Robert McKendrick, pp. 1, 8, 22, 29, 30, 34, 36, 42, 72; A. Paul Mouw, pp. 20, 53, 66.

Library of Congress Catalog Card Number: 73-85963

ISBN 0-87788-969-4

Printed in the United States of America

90 89 88 87 86 85 84 83   5 4 3 2 1

Contents

	A Word to Parents	6
1	Living means growing	9
2	Growing means changing	23
3	You're getting there!	37
4	Partners and parents	47
5	A new life begins	57
6	Talking together	67
	Glossary	77

A Word to Parents:
This book is an attempt to relate to children between the ages nine and thirteen the wonderful story of human sexuality. In a time when our children are being bombarded from every direction with sexual information, it's more important than ever that parents communicate effectively with their children.

Nothing I can write will adequately take the place of a positive, informative discussion between you and your child regarding sex.

Hopefully this book can be used as a tool, but it cannot do the job alone. You will want to explain sex to your child in your own words.

May I suggest that you read this book first, then give it to your child to read. Hopefully, interaction between the two of you will follow.

Keep in mind one important fact. The information you give your child regarding sex will not be nearly as important as the attitude with which you present that information. Your own attitudes and relationships in the family will be passed on to your child. He will listen to your words but he will *copy* your attitudes.

Correct facts but unhealthy attitudes can only result in a faulty if not negative sex education of your child. A combination of correct information, positive attitudes and a basic appreciation to God for giving us our human bodies—so wonderfully made with such potential for joy and health and beauty —will lead to healthy sex education for your child.

As well as the information in the text, a glossary has been included at the end of the book to define clearly all the terms printed *in italics*. Guides to pronunciation have also been provided.

We hope that this will simplify and help the learning and sharing of vital information for parent and child.

—*Mary Kehle, M.A., R.N.*

Living means growing

1

All living things must grow. When growth stops, your life stops. Even when you reach your full height, the cells in your body are constantly being replaced. Thus growth continues. Plant a daisy seed in the ground. First a tiny sprout pushes through the dirt. Then a few leaves develop and finally a beautiful bloom appears. Through growth, the seed has become a lovely flower and as long as it lives, it will continue to grow and produce new leaves and flowers.

Watch a baby bird or a new kitten or a wobbly, clumsy calf. They too must grow. If they don't, we worry because we know something is wrong. We know it is neither natural nor healthy. All newborn animals must change and develop and grow.

Like the plants and animals, God has made you a growing organism. He does not intend for you to always stay the same. Rather, he has planned that your body and mind will gradually change from that of a baby to that of an adult.

A good example

The Bible gives us a very good example of how God wants young people to grow and mature. In Luke 2:39-52 (*New English Bible*) we are given a look into Jesus' life when he was twelve years old (the same age as many of you!) By studying this short passage, we not only see how Jesus developed into a mature person but we also have a good guide-line to use for ourselves. In verse 39, Luke says that Jesus grew "big and strong". Often when we picture Jesus in our minds, we see him either as a tiny baby in a manger or as a grown man, hanging on a cross. But here we are told about him as he was at the age of twelve. Having gone through the baby and toddler stage, then the early school years, he was now about to become a teenager. Physically, he was maturing.

Verse 39 tells us that in addition to growing physically, Jesus was also "full of wisdom". He had matured mentally or intellectually. In the days when Jesus was a child, boys usually began to attend school at the synagogue (Jewish Church) at age six. Though we're not told so specifically in the

Bible, it is probably safe to assume that Jesus went to school like other little Jewish boys. In addition to any education he might have received at school, he also learned from his father, a carpenter, his godly mother, Mary and from the teachers and priests at the synagogue.

Physical and mental growth were not enough, however. Verse 52 of the same chapter says that Jesus also "grew in favor with God". He studied and learned much about God in his young years and he was always concerned about God's will for his life. Even as a child he trusted in God. Of course, Jesus was more than just a child, he was also the Son of God. In fact, he *was* God. Throughout his childhood and as an adult, Jesus lived in the closest harmony possible with God. He was a spiritually mature person. We also should aim to become spiritually "grown up". A close relationship with God through Christ will make us mature.

Finally we see that as Jesus matured, "he grew in favor with men". This seems to say that Jesus got along well with other people. He understood them, spent time with them and loved them. He was kind and helpful to others. Rather than being afraid or nervous with other people Jesus was at ease with everyone he met. Putting it into our words today, we would say that he matured socially.

Just from this short story in Luke we can see at least *four ways in which God wants us to grow and mature:* physically, intellectually, spiritually and socially.

How your body grows
To develop in these ways, however, takes time. Many things must happen before you will be a mature man or woman. In this chapter we want to take a closer look at how our bodies have been created. This will help you understand how a boy or girl matures physically.

When you were born some ten or twelve years ago, you had the body of an infant. That body was made up of many wonderful systems. Your heart, blood vessels and lungs made up your circulatory and respiratory systems. You also had a digestive system which included your stomach and intestines. Another system present in your body was the reproductive. It consisted of those organs which were necessary to help you reproduce or give birth to a child some time much later in your life. It is this system that we want to take a closer look at now. Because girls' and boys' reproductive organs are very different, we'll study them separately.

First we want to consider the reproductive or sexual organs of a girl. You will find it easier to understand if you look at the illustrations as you read.

A girl's sexual organs
Lying in the lower abdomen (the area you

often call your stomach) is the girl's reproductive system. At birth, these organs are very small. Located on either side of her abdomen are two almond shaped organs called the *ovaries* which hold thousands of tiny eggs, called *ova* or female sex cells. These are so small they cannot be seen with the naked eye. Not actually attached to the ovaries, but lying very close by are the *fallopian tubes.* These tubes have a hollow inside no larger than a pencil lead. At one end the tubes connect to the uterus. At the other end, the tubes spread out, fingerlike and each seems to reach out toward an ovary.

The uterus lies quite low in the middle of the abdomen behind the pubic bone that forms a bridge-like connection between a girl's two legs. It is a pear shaped organ, hollow on the inside with very thick walls which are made up of muscle. The top part of the uterus is rounded. Then it tapers down to a very small opening at the bottom of the uterus which we call the *cervix*. Leading from the cervix to the outside of the body is a passageway called the *vagina*. The outside opening of the vagina is located between the *urethra* (the opening from which urine passes) and the *anus* (the opening from which feces or a bowel movement passes). These three openings (also called orifices) are protected by two soft folds of flesh and skin which cover this whole sensitive genital area. Those folds are called the *labia*. Also protected by the labia is a small pea shaped organ called the *clitoris*. It is located just above the urethra and is very sensitive.

When discussing the sexual organs of a woman or little girl, we must also include the *breasts* which are flat and without shape in a little girl. The nipple is pinkish gray in color. In young children, the breasts of boys and girls look exactly alike.

With the help of this illustration and re-

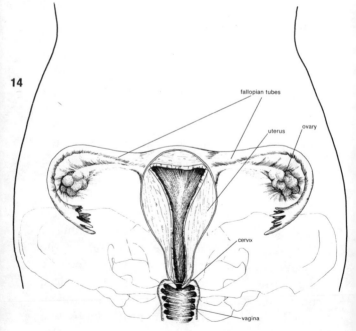

FEMALE SEX ORGANS

membering what you've read so far, you should now know where a girl's sexual organs are and what they are called.

Can you remember?

Take this quick matching test and see how much you remember. Find the best definition of the following words from the list below and match each number to a word:

_____ orifice   _____ vagina

_____ anus   _____ fallopian tubes

_____ abdomen   _____ labia

15

_____ urethra   _____ ovaries

1. two folds of skin and flesh which protect sensitive organs underneath.
2. tubes leading from the uterus to the ovaries.
3. opening
4. area of body commonly referred to as stomach.
5. passageway leading from the cervix to outside of body.
6. opening through which urine passes.
7. two almond shaped organs lying on either side of uterus.
8. opening through which feces passes.

Check your answers to quizzes on page 80.

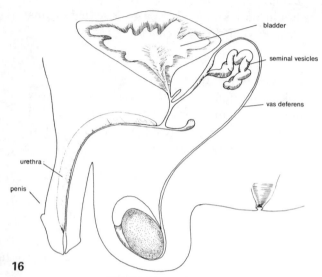

bladder

seminal vesicles

vas deferens

urethra

penis

16

MALE SEX ORGANS (SIDE VIEW)

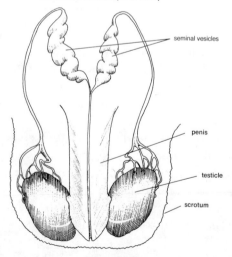

seminal vesicles

penis

testicle

scrotum

MALE SEX ORGANS (FRONT VIEW)

A boy's sexual organs

Unlike the girl's sexual organs which are located mainly inside her lower abdomen, the boy's reproductive organs are outside the body.

Boys have two small, oval shaped organs which produce the male sex cells or *sperm*. We call these organs the *testicles*. The sperm are smaller than the female egg. They have tiny tails on them and look like tadpoles. The sperm cannot survive in too warm a temperature. That is why the testicles are contained in a sac made of loose skin. This sac, called the *scrotum*, hangs between a boy's legs, close to his body. If the testicles were inside the boy's body, the warm body temperature might kill 17 the sperm.

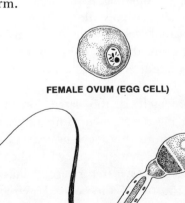

FEMALE OVUM (EGG CELL)

MALE SPERM CELL

The sperm do not stay in the testicles. They must travel out of the body and one sperm cell meet with the woman's ovum in order to begin a new life. This process is called *conception*. A series of tiny tubes carry the sperm from the testicles up into the *seminal vesicles* where the sperm are mixed with a whitish fluid. The fluid and the sperm combined are called *semen*. The semen then passes through another small tube called the urethra and out the body. This is the same opening from which urine passes but semen and urine do not pass from the urethra at the same time.

Hanging in front of the scrotum is a finger-like organ called the *penis*. Located at the tip of the penis is the urethra. Urine is passed through this opening. At birth, a loose fold of skin covers the end of the penis. In many cases, parents choose to have this skin removed before the new baby leaves the hospital. This minor surgery is called *circumcision*.

Can you picture someone putting on a sweater which is too large for him? The sleeves hang right down to his finger tips. He has to push up the sleeve in order to free his hand. A boy's penis is somewhat like this. The skin, like the sweater sleeve, hangs loosely around the tip of the penis. To circumcise a boy, the doctor pushes up the skin, like the sleeve of a sweater and then removes the extra skin. When finished, the tip of the penis or *glans* is exposed (as the hand is exposed after you push up the sleeve of the sweater).

You have probably read of circumcision in the Bible. Back in Old Testament times, God required circumcision of all Jewish boys when they were eight days old. This act served as a physical sign to show that the Jewish boys were part of God's chosen people.

Today circumcision is usually done for hygenic or medical reasons. One important reason for circumcision is that the penis may then be kept clean more easily.

The penis normally hangs limp but can at times become firm. Then it extends at an angle from the body. When this happens we say the penis is erect or that the boy has an *erection*.

Tissues within the penis are in some ways like a sponge. Under certain conditions, blood

UNCIRCUMCISED PENIS

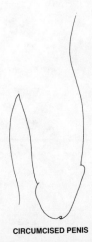

CIRCUMCISED PENIS

flows rapidly into the penis and like a full sponge, it becomes enlarged. The veins which normally carry the blood away from the penis are closed off. Because the blood is trapped within the spongy tissues of the penis, it becomes firm and erect. Many things can cause a boy to have an erection. Sometimes it is due to tight clothing or a full bladder. It can also be caused by sexual excitement or by handling of the penis. Whatever the cause, a penis will not remain erect for long. Don't be concerned about it. It will soon return to its normal position.

God put it all together

Whether you are a boy or girl, your body was created by God. Sometimes children are

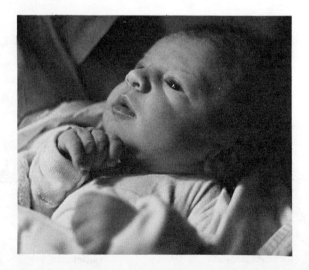

born with physical or mental handicaps. Usually, however, such handicaps are not present. Regardless of outward appearances, you are a beautiful and valuable person to God and those who love you. God desires that all children grow and mature and reach their highest potential. David understood what a wonderful creation our bodies are when he said in Psalm 139:13, 14, "You (God) made all the delicate, inner parts of my body, and knit them together in my mother's womb. Thank you for making me so wonderfully complex! It is amazing to think about. Your workmanship is marvelous—and how well I know it."

Now you are in that age group when you can expect to see new changes taking place in your body. This process we call physical maturing. This is a big part of growing up.

Let's review!

Here's a quiz for boys. Find the right words to fill in the blanks:

1. The two male sex organs which produce sperm are _____.

2. When a boy's penis becomes filled with blood and is firm, we say the boy has an _____.

3. A whitish fluid containing sperm is called _____.

4. The sac containing the testicles is called the _____.

5. The tube through which both urine and semen passes is called the _____.

Growing
means
changing

Growth begins when a new life is first conceived and continues until death. This happens so naturally that we often don't realize how complex our bodies really are. All of the systems inside us work together to keep us living—and growing. The system which is "in charge" of the overall functioning of our bodies is the endocrine or hormonal system.

How hormones help us

The endocrine system is made up of six glands, but we will discuss only those which are directly involved in reproduction.

Located in the head, just below the brain, is the *pituitary* gland. It acts like the "Officer in command", sending messages to other glands throughout the body. The pituitary tells the ovaries and testicles when to begin sending out their secretions (*hormones*) which will start the development of male and female traits. It also tells the ovaries and testicles when to begin producing and releasing eggs and sperm (usually somewhere between ages ten and fourteen).

Another important gland is the *thyroid*. It is located in the neck close to the larynx or voicebox. This gland influences the development and growth of our bodies.

If you remember, we discussed the ovaries and testicles in chapter one. These too are glands and produce hormones which bring about certain changes (such as breast development in girls and growth of a beard in boys). Sometimes we call the ovaries and testicles the "sex glands" or "*gonads*".

As these glands begin to secrete their hormones into your body, the first signs of *puberty* appear.

Puberty (sometimes called *adolescence*) refers to that time in a boy or girl's life when he or she is first capable of reproducing life. Put another way, puberty is when a young person's reproductive organs mature enough to function. When you were a young child, say four or five, you could not have children of your own. It would have been absolutely impossible. However, somewhere between ten and your early teen years, your body became capable of reproducing life. Of course, it is not at all wise to have a baby at such a young age, but it is possible. It does seem clear that much more is needed to be a good mother or father than simply being able to give birth. A young person needs his teenage years to mature emotionally, socially and spiritually so that later he or she will be fully able to assume the responsibilities of parenthood.

Growing up girls

Girls begin to mature a little sooner than boys. Around age ten or eleven (though it may be as early as age nine or not until thirteen or fourteen) some physical changes will begin taking place.

The breasts will change first. The nipples will begin to darken in color and then the tissue around the nipple will look slightly puffy. Gradually, usually over a period of several years, the breasts will begin to take the shape and form of those of a woman. Of course, not all girls will develop at the same rate. At age twelve, one girl's breasts may be much smaller than another girl's. This may worry her but she should not be too concerned. As the rest of her body grows, the breasts will also develop. By the time she has reached adulthood, her breasts will usually be well proportioned to the rest of her body.

As breast development continues, a girl may want to wear a training bra. Later on a firmer bra can be worn both for support and protection.

Along with breast development, hair will begin to grow under the arms and in a triangular patch over the pubic bone. Often a girl will wish to shave the hair under the arms for neater grooming and to help prevent perspiration odor. However, she should ask her mother for help the first time. A razor is sharp and it takes practice to learn how to use one safely. There is no need at all to shave the pubic hair.

The hair on a girl's legs also becomes darker and more noticeable, especially if she is a brunette. Many girls may want to begin shaving their legs at this time.

In addition, her hips will begin to fill out and become more rounded. This, along with the breast development, gives her a lovely, curved body compared to the more slender hipped, flat chested boy.

Anywhere from six months to two years after the appearance of pubic and underarm hair, she can expect to have her first menstrual period. This is a discharge of blood from the vagina. It will happen every month and last for several days. We will discuss menstruation in more detail in the following chapter.

Both boys and girls may notice changes in their skin at this time. Some pimples and blackheads may appear on the face and the skin may become more oily. This condition is called acne and is very common among adolescents. In some cases, medical care might be required but often careful cleansing of the face and neck will help minimize the problem.

It is not wise to pick or squeeze pimples. This may lead to an infection which in turn may leave scars. If a young person has a particularly bad skin problem, a skin doctor or dermatologist should be consulted. He will be able to give advice and medical help.

Acne may last several years. However, as the hormone levels in the body become more stable, acne usually disappears.

True or False
1. Another word for puberty is pituitary. _____
2. The ovaries and testicles secrete hormones.

   _____
3. There are six glands in the reproductive system. _____

4. Breast development begins before the appearance of underarm and pubic hair. _____
5. Menstrual periods begin approximately six months before breast development begins.

   _____

As a boy gets bigger
Boys enter puberty about one year later than girls, somewhere between ages eleven and fourteen. There is usually no change in a boy's breasts. However, he too will have growth of hair under his arms and in the pubic area and perhaps later on his chest. In addition, soft, light hair will appear on his face and upper lip. In time, this hair will become darker and coarser and it will be necessary to shave. Most boys look forward to this.

It is a sign that they are growing up.

Voice changes occur, too. Before adolescence, a boy's voice sounds much like a girl's. Then it begins to get deeper. As the vocal cords grow and stretch, a boy's voice may slide up and down. It may also crack right in the middle of a sentence. This happens even though he is trying to speak in a normal voice. Sometimes it's embarrassing! But in a year or two most boys will have a rich, deep voice.

A boy's sexual organs are changing at this time too. Usually around twelve or thirteen he will notice a "growth spurt" and the penis and scrotum will grow larger and resemble those of his father. Since boys do not all experience this "growth spurt" at the same time, their sexual organs may not look alike at the same age. This might worry a boy. While taking a shower after gym glass, he may compare himself to others and be concerned. He need not be. Each boy matures at his own rate and his rate of development is just right for him.

When a boy has his first wet dream or *nocturnal emission* (a discharge of semen from the penis while he is asleep), he knows that his body is now producing sperm. We will discuss wet dreams in more detail in the next chapter.

True or False

1. Voice changes occur because the vocal cords are growing and stretching. _____

2. Boys usually mature before girls. _____
3. Another name for wet dream is nocturnal emission. _____
4. Most boys and girls are unable to become parents before age eighteen. _____
5. A skin condition often found in both boys and girls during puberty is acne. _____

Changing viewpoints

In addition to physical changes during adolescence, both boys and girls will experience

new and varied feelings. Things which you used to enjoy doing may seem babyish to you now. Not long ago it was fun playing house or having tea parties with a little sister. Boys, you didn't mind playing with cars on the living room rug with your smaller brother. Somehow, those things aren't so enjoyable anymore.

Perhaps you also get more easily upset. You may find yourself crying or becoming frustrated over things that never bothered you before. You may become irritable and cranky without really knowing why. All of a sudden, it seems as if an awful lot is expected from you. Your list of chores at home gets longer and longer.

At school, teachers are also beginning to demand more from you. They expect you to sit still for long periods of time. There are fewer recesses; more special assignments. Homework increases. Responsibilities grow. Everywhere, people expect more. Sometimes it seems very unfair and you wish you could be little again.

You've probably all said at one time or another, "I wish I were just a little kid again. I wouldn't have to do any work, just play all day". But remember, small children have their problems too. They must still take naps and they have to stay in mother's sight every minute. If little brother goes into his room and shuts the door, mother is soon checking on him to see if he's "into anything". Small children have very little freedom or privacy. And though they have few responsibilities, they have even fewer privileges! This part of growing up, with all its new feelings and responsibilities, it is an important part of God's plan for your life. He will use these experiences to help you become a mature, happy person.

Probably the best way to handle these confused feelings is to talk with someone about them. Your mother or dad want to share this part of your life with you. After all, they were young once too, and have had many of these same feelings. Confide in them. Tell them what's bothering you. Ask them the things you don't understand. Your parents very often will be able to help you.

Sometimes you may not really know why you are feeling a certain way. If Mom asks you, "Why are you so cranky today?", you may have to answer, "I really don't know why, Mom. I just am". That is an honest answer. Somewhere inside, you may feel misunderstood or hurt or perhaps you feel you've been unfairly punished. Or maybe you think that list of chores Mom gave you to do for the week is just too long. And so you feel cranky. But, you can't really put your finger on the reason why. However, after listening to you a minute, Mom may say, "Do you suppose you're irritable and cranky today because I scolded you yesterday for not cleaning up your room? Maybe you think I was being too fussy; maybe you think I was unfair. Could we talk about it?" (Ah! Somewhere deep inside, that rings a bell!! You *did* feel irritated when she made such a fuss over your room. You even went to bed a little angry and this morning when you woke up you had a good case of the "grumps".)

"Boy, Mom. You may be right. Yes—I did feel you were unfair-----". And then a surprising thing happens. After talking about the problem with Mom for a few minutes, you suddenly start to feel better. Maybe she understands after all and well—"maybe my room was kind of a mess."

The grumps disappear! By talking out the problem you feel much better.

Feeling mad?

Closely related to grumpy feelings are angry feelings. However, we often find it harder to admit we're angry. Grumpy—maybe. But angry? Not me. I'm not mad. I'M NOT MAD!

Why is it so hard to admit we're mad sometimes? One reason is that we often feel that it is wrong—even sinful—to get angry. But is this really what the Bible teaches? You might be surprised to know that the Lord Jesus got angry at times. In Mark 3:1-5 Jesus met a man with a deformed hand. Since it was the Sabbath, some of Jesus' enemies watched him closely to see whether or not he would heal the man. If Jesus healed him, the enemies would say that Jesus had broken the Sabbath.

In verse five it says that Jesus became *angry* because they were so "indifferent to human need." Those men just didn't care about the needs of the injured man.

Jesus had a good reason for getting angry. He was angry with cruel or unjust people. There are times when you may have a good reason for getting angry. However, we must all be careful that we don't get angry over every little thing.

God himself certainly became angry at times. But the Bible makes it clear that he was very *slow* to get angry. Psalms 103:8 says, "He is merciful and tender towards those who don't deserve it; he is *slow* to get angry and full of kindness and love. We too should be patient and loving with other people. And

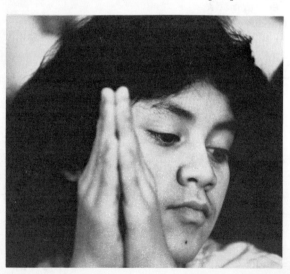

hopefully, we too will be "slow to get angry".

Perhaps one of the most important things to remember about anger is found in Ephesians 4:26 where it says, "If you are angry, don't sin by nursing your grudge. Don't let the sun go down with you still angry—get over it quickly".

In other words, find out why you're angry and work the problem out. Don't let it build up inside you until you explode! If you get over your anger before you go to bed you'll not only be obeying the Bible, but you'll also sleep better!

Again, probably the best way to handle your angry feelings is to talk about them. If you know whom you are angry at, go to that person and, as gently as possible, tell them why you are mad. Then listen to *his* or *her* side of the story. Together you can often work the problem out.

If you are angry at someone or some situation but it's impossible to go to the person involved, then discuss it with someone else, like a parent or teacher or good friend. Also, be sure to tell the Lord you're upset; he can help calm your anger and give you peace. Angry feelings must be brought out into the open and talked about and prayed over. They can't be left smoldering somewhere inside you. That simply doesn't solve any problems.

Feelings that bother you, (sadness, anger, fear or the "grumps") are best handled by sharing them with someone who cares. When you do you'll find you feel a hundred percent better!

God is vitally interested in you during this changing time of your life. While your parents and friends may be good listeners and be willing to help you solve your problems, God alone can give you the *power* to change. Since he created you to begin with, he can understand how you are feeling and he has promised to help.

"Let him (God) have all your worries and cares, for he is always thinking about you and watching everything that concerns you."

3

Something exciting is about to happen! Or maybe it has already happened in your life.

Usually somewhere between ages nine and fourteen a girl has her first menstrual period and a boy his first wet dream. These are important events. They show that a girl's ovaries are now sending out egg cells and a boy's testicles are producing sperm. It is at this time that a young person enters that stage of his life called puberty. Among some groups of people, this is considered to be an extremely important day. Certain public rituals are practiced and a great deal of emphasis is placed on the first menstrual period or wet dream.

In our culture, though we do not make a public announcement about these things, they are still important. In some homes a girl is allowed some special treat or new privilege when she has her first menstrual period. Or a boy may be given a special gift or taken on an outing with his father when he experiences his first wet dream. This is one way that parents can say, "We are proud of you and we're glad that you're growing up. This *is* an important day!"

What exactly happens during a menstrual period or wet dream? We'll begin first with menstruation.

Menstruation

The story of menstruation begins in the ovaries (see illustration 1). Contained within the ovaries are thousands of tiny egg cells (so small they can't be seen with the naked eye). Each month one of these eggs goes to the surface of the ovary where it is contained in a small sac called the *follicle*. The follicle looks like a tiny blister on the surface of the ovary.

The follicle then breaks and the egg cell is released to begin its journey down the fallopian tube. After a girl reaches puberty, this happens every 28 to 32 days. Usually only one ovary produces an egg each month. We call the monthly release of an egg *ovulation*.

After the egg cell leaves the ovary, it travels down the fallopian tube into the uterus. The lining of the uterus is thick and contains many blood vessels. If the girl were pregnant, it would provide a safe and nourishing place for the baby to grow. But if the girl is not pregnant, the special lining in the uterus is not needed and it begins to separate from the uterus. The egg, extra tissue and blood drain out of the uterus through the vagina. This drainage of blood from the vagina is called menstruation. When a girl is menstruating, we often say she is having a "period".

Menstrual periods occur about once a month and last between three and five days. However, when a girl first begins menstruating, her periods may be somewhat irregular. She may even skip a month or two. Later on she will probably have very regular periods and will be able to predict when to expect menstruation each month.

Menstruation is a very normal process. It is not a sickness and a girl does not have to avoid any of her regular activities during this time. Sometimes she may experience some mild cramping in the lower abdomen. It more severe cramping develops, she should see a doctor.

Years ago, before people really understood much about menstruation, some women did have rather mistaken ideas about periods. They believed that it was harmful to swim or bathe while menstruating. They also thought physical activities were bad for them and they might even go to bed for the four or five day period. Think of all they missed while lying in bed, believing they were sick! We know now that all that was very unnecessary. Most girls are able to do everything during a menstrual period that they would do otherwise.

The average menstrual flow will amount to about four to six tablespoons of blood. Since this happens over a period of three to five days, only small amounts of blood will be lost each day.

To prevent a girl's clothing from becoming stained some type of protection must be used. A sanitary pad is one way in which the menstrual blood can be collected. The pad is made of an absorbent material. Worn between the legs, it attaches to the girl's panties by an adhesive material on the back of the pad. The pad is changed whenever necessary, usually three or four times a day.

Some girls prefer using tampons instead of sanitary pads. A tampon is a small, tight roll of absorbent material which is inserted into the vagina. Tampons should be changed several times a day. This greatly reduces the risk of developing an illness called Toxic Shock Syndrome.

Usually when a girl first begin having periods, she uses pads but may decide later that tampons are more convenient. She should ask her mother or doctor about how to insert one properly.

It is especially important that a girl either bathe or wash the genital area every day during a period. This will help eliminate any bothersome odors.

A special word to girls: It would be very

wise to discuss menstruation with your mother *before* you actually begin having periods. Usually, your mother will bring the subject up first and give you an opportunity to ask questions. She will show you how to use a sanitary pad or tampon. It's a good idea for you either to keep these items in your room (even though you don't need them yet) or know where your mother keeps them. You just might start your period sometime when your mother is not at home. If you know where to find a pad and how to use it, you will be able to manage alone until your mother gets home. Then you probably will want to share this important happening with her.

You may be wondering what you should do with a used sanitary pad. It should not be put in the toilet. It can be wrapped in toilet paper, paper toweling, or some other material and placed in a waste can. In most public restrooms, there are small containers, clearly marked, just for this purpose. Tampons may be disposed of in the toilet. They are much smaller and will not present a plumbing problem.

Some girls tell of a special problem they have at school. The toilets there do not always have doors. Or, the doors may be without latches. This makes it difficult to have privacy. If you are unable to find a private place at school where you can change a pad or tampon, report this to your school nurse or your gym teacher. She should be able to help you with this situation.

When you first begin having periods, you may feel a little self-conscious about it, especially if you are one of the first girls in your class to menstruate. Just remember, all girls have periods sooner or later. You may think that everyone can tell when you're menstruating. They can't! It's your own secret unless you choose to share it with a special friend. Soon, all of your friends will have begun their periods too, and it will just be a normal part of your lives.

Do you remember?
1. Where the egg cell is produced?

2. What the monthly release of an egg is called?

3. How the egg gets to the uterus?
4. How often girls usually have a period?
5. Another word used for describing periods?
6. How long a period usually lasts?

Nocturnal emissions

Somewhere between ages twelve and fourteen most boys will experience a "wet dream" or "nocturnal emission". Wet dreams simply refer to the release of semen through the penis while a boy is sleeping. Usually he will have been dreaming. In the dream, he will often be with a girl. Perhaps he is dreaming that he likes the girl very much. He may put his arms around her or kiss her. While dreaming this, the boy's penis will become erect. As the dream continues, semen will be released or ejaculated through the penis. At the time of ejaculation, the boy will be aware of a very pleasurable feeling in his genital area.

Often he will awaken at this time. He may feel a little strange or even guilty about what has happened. But there is no reason to worry about wet dreams. He has no control over them. This is the natural way of getting rid of extra semen which the body has produced. Though not every boy will have wet dreams, most will. Unlike a girl's periods, which occur regularly, wet dreams do not follow any time schedule. Some boys may experience them much more often than others.

Sometimes parents forget to tell boys about wet dreams before they happen. Then when it does occur, the boy may be worried and upset. How can he explain to Mom the soiled pajamas? If Mom or Dad are wise, they will explain wet dreams to their sons just as they explained menstruation to their daughters. Also Mom might tell her son, "Don't worry about your pajamas when you have a wet dream. Just get up and change and then go back to sleep".

While you may want to share this experience with your Dad or Mom the first time it happens, it is not necessary to tell them about it each time. They understand that this will be a normal part of your life. They will be glad to know that you are maturing and becoming a man.

Keeping the balance

During this time boys (and sometimes girls) find it hard to know how to handle their sexual feelings. A young person may find himself spending a great deal of time "thinking about sex." Perhaps he goes looking for books and pictures which will excite him sexually as he looks at them. There's also a real tendency for him to want to "daydream" about sexual feelings. Rather than talking about his sexual feelings with someone like a parent or doctor and having his questions answered that way, the young person just imagines all sorts of things in his mind—many of which often aren't true.

To think and wonder and read about sex isn't wrong. Most doctors or teachers or parents can suggest good books for a young person to read when he is interested in knowing more about his body and its functions. These same people are also usually willing to listen to and answer any questions he or she might have regarding sex. However, to spend many minutes alone each day just thinking about sex will surely take away from a young person's time which could be spent at more fun and rewarding things like sports, crafts, time with friends, wholesome reading, special projects, etc. In fact, becoming very busy in other activities will help him to keep the proper balance between time spent thinking about sexual things and time spent in other important activities.

Again, the Bible gives us some very practical help in dealing with thoughts and feelings.

David says in I Chronicles 28:9 ". . . my son, *get to know* the *God* of your fathers. Worship and serve him with a clean heart and a willing mind, for the Lord sees every heart and *understands and knows* every thought". David goes on to say in Psalm 139:23, 24, "Search me, O God, and know my heart; test my thoughts. Point out anything you find in me that makes you sad, and lead me along the path of everlasting life".

Quiz:

1. The release of semen through the penis is called _____ .

2. Another name for "wet dreams" is _____ _____ .

3. Most boys experience wet dreams between ages _____ and _____ .

4

What makes human families different from animal "families"? We often talk about a mother and father cat and their kittens as a family, yet we know that this isn't really true. Usually the father cat leaves the mother cat right after mating. Then when the kittens are able to live alone, the mother leaves also. Six months later the mother cat may have kittens but this time with a different father! Yet, there is nothing wrong with this. God has created the animals to live this way. He didn't plan for cats to have permanent "families".

However, when God made us, he had something quite different in mind. The Bible tells us that people are to be "committed" or "promised" to one another before they have babies. This means finding one person whom we love and with whom we want to spend our lives. We then go through a legal ceremony (often performed in a church) and are married. The husband and wife now make up a family. Into this family children may be born. If the parents love each other and are committed to each other, the children have a safe and secure place in which to grow and mature. Sometimes, however, parents decide to separate or divorce and the children may feel very sad and disappointed. They may even feel it is their fault that the parents have separated. This is not true! Rather, parents have found it impossible to live together happily. Though they may no longer love each other, they almost always continue to love their children very much.

Marriage in the Bible

The Bible places great importance on marriage and the family. In Mark 10:7-9 Jesus says, "For from the very first he (God) made man and woman to be joined together permanently in marriage; therefore a man is to leave his father and mother, and he and his wife are united so that they are no longer two, but one".

Marriage is one of the most important family relationships planned and approved of by God. In the New Testament Paul speaks of a Christian's relationship to Christ as being *like* a marriage. If marriage can be compared to Christ's relationship with us then surely we can't afford to make light of it.

Not all people will marry. In Scripture, the apostle Paul is a good example of a man who probably never married, yet accomplished many great things for God.

Some people just seem to get along better in life without a marriage partner. Maybe their life's work is so demanding that they would not have time to care for a husband or wife and children. Others may feel that they have never met a man or woman whom they would like to marry. Rather than live with just anyone, perhaps very unhappily, they choose not to marry at all. Some decide to remain single because they think they would be happiest that way. You don't have to be married to be happy! The apostle Paul gives good advice in I Corinthians 7:17 when he says, "But be sure in deciding these matters that you are living as God intended, marrying or not marrying in accordance with God's direction and help, and accepting whatever situation God has put you into".

Most of you, however, will marry someday. Though more and more people are marrying while they are still teenagers, it's very important not to rush into marriage. Your teen years are exciting ones and there is still so much for you to do and learn. Even though most teenagers are fully developed sexually, they are still growing—emotionally, socially and spiritually.

Getting together

To help in emotional and social growth, most of you will want to date. Dating is not only fun, it is important. It's natural for boys and girls to want to be together. At first, it is probably easier and wiser to go out in groups. Several fellows and girls may be together to a church party or a school football game. As you become older and more confident, you'll want to go out alone with your date. Unfortunately, not all parents and their children agree on what age a young person should begin dating. Because each case is different, you must work this out with your own parents. As they see signs of responsibility and trustworthiness in you, they will be willing to allow you to begin dating. How you feel is important too. You will probably not want to begin dating until you feel reasonably comfortable with those of the opposite sex.

Dating usually continues throughout the teen years into the early twenties. Many young adults will then marry, although some people wait many years before marrying. *When* you marry is not nearly so important as *whom* you marry. As a Christian, you can expect God to help you make this very important decision.

Starting a family

After you marry, you may decide that you would like children of your own. We already know that within the man's and woman's bodies are the sperm and egg necessary to produce new life. But how do the sperm and egg meet?

Let's refresh our memories a bit. We know that the egg cell begins its journey from the woman's ovary. It travels through the fallopian tube, into the uterus and eventually leaves the body through the vagina.

In the man, the sperm are produced in the testicles. They travel through a tiny tube, are combined with a whitish fluid and ejaculated or discharged through the penis. In each release of semen from the penis, there are millions of sperm, not just one.

How do the sperm and egg meet? It's really quite simple. God has created us so that the husband's penis, after becoming firm and erect, fits right into the wife's vagina. This act is called *sexual intercourse.* During intercourse the sperm leave the man's body and are deposited in the woman's vagina. The little "tails" on the sperm help them to travel up the uterus and into the fallopian tube. If the woman's ovary has released an egg cell, it too will have moved into the fallopian tube. There, just one of the sperm will unite with the egg. All the others quickly die. We call this uniting of the egg and sperm *conception* or *fertilization.*

Following conception, the egg cell begins to multiply. The one cell becomes two, the two become four, the four become eight, and so on. Five to seven days later, the egg will have moved down the tube and into the uterus. There it attaches itself to the lining, which has become soft and velvety. For nine months, or approximately 266 days, the egg cells will continue to divide and slowly the new baby will develop.

You may be wondering how often a couple has intercourse and whether or not a woman becomes pregnant each time. Because intercourse is a happy and pleasurable experience for the husband and wife, they may experience it whenever they wish. A woman will not become pregnant each time she has intercourse since her ovaries release an egg cell only once a month (ovulation). Also, there are various ways of preventing pregnancy if a husband and wife wish not to have a baby. We refer to this as practicing birth control.

Boy, or girl?

What will the new baby look like? Will it be a boy or girl? The answer to these questions

and many more lie within a thread-like particle called a chromosome. At the time of conception, the woman's egg and the man's sperm each contain 23 chromosomes. Within the chromosomes are genes. Genes determine what a baby will look like—the color of his skin, hair and eyes, his height, the shape of his nose, ears and mouth and other physical traits. Each new baby will be a unique new person. He may resemble his parents or a brother or sister but he will actually be different from anyone else because the combination of chromosomes and genes within him will be unlike those in any other person.

Chromosomes also determine the sex of a new baby. There are actually two kinds of sperm. One is called an X chromosome sperm, the other a Y chromosome sperm. If an X chromosome sperm unites with the woman's egg, the baby will be a girl. If a Y chromosome sperm fertilizes the egg, the baby will be a boy.

Perhaps you've wondered what causes twins? In some cases, when one egg was fertilized by one sperm, the egg divided completely in two and two babies began to grow rather than just one. We call these babies "identical twins" because they are always of the same sex and look very much alike. In fact you might not be able to tell them apart.

At other times, the woman's ovary produces two eggs instead of the usual one. If the two eggs are fertilized by two sperm, "fraternal twins" will result. They may be of the same sex, or they may be a boy and a girl. Since fraternal twins result from the fertilization of two separate eggs, there is no more reason for these twins to look alike than any two children born into a family at different times.

In the United States twins occur about once in every 88 births. It's also possible for a woman to give birth to three or four or sometimes even more babies at one time, although this happens very infrequently.

Review:

1. The uniting of the sperm and egg is called
   _____ or _____ .

2. The act by which the sperm are deposited in the vagina is called _____ .
3. The fertilized egg will move from the fallopian tube into the uterus about _____ days after conception.
4. The time from conception until birth is _____ months.
5. The sperm and egg each contain _____ chromosomes.
6. The physical traits of the new baby are determined by _____ .
7. If an X chromosome unites with the egg, the new baby will be a _____ .
8. If two eggs are fertilized by two sperm, _____ twins will result.
9. Identical twins will always be of the _____ sex.

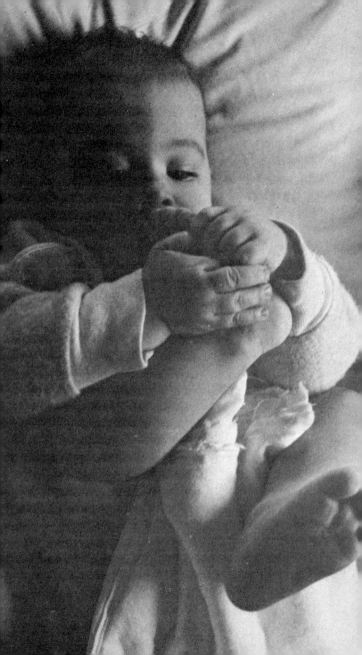

5

In chapter four we discovered how the male sperm and female egg meet. The fertilized egg then travels down into the uterus where the new baby begins to grow. When this happens we say that the woman is pregnant.

Pregnancy can be a very thrilling part of a woman's life. What could be more exciting for her than to know that a miracle is taking place in her own body? We cannot understand this miracle completely, but there is a lot we do know.

Remember that about five to seven days after conception, the cluster of egg cells moves into the uterus where it attaches itself to the lining. There the cells continue to divide and grow. A short time later they become enclosed in a small sac. The sac is filled with fluid called *amniotic fluid*. As the baby grows, the sac also grows and the amount of fluid increases. The purpose of the amniotic fluid is to help protect the new baby.

Have you ever tried to "spank" a playmate while under water? If so, you know that you can't do it very well. The water gets in your way. You can't move your hand fast or hard enough through the water to really hurt anyone.

The amniotic fluid does the same thing. If the mother falls or is accidently bumped, the fluid cushions the baby and keeps him from being hurt. Actually the baby floats in the fluid. Sometimes this sac of fluid is called the "bag of waters".

For the first seven or eight weeks of the baby's life, he is called an embryo. By five weeks, the embryo is only about ¼ inch long but it already has a brain, spinal cord and a very faint heartbeat.

By the end of the second month, fingers, toes, ears, and eyes have begun to form. The embryo also has a complete skeleton though it is made of cartilage, not bone (cartilage is the rubbery material found in your ears and the tip of your nose). The embryo is now about one inch long and weighs one-thirtieth of an ounce.

By the beginning of the third month, the embryo is called a *fetus*. During this month, the fetus grows faster and true bone cells are formed. In the fourth month, the toenails and teeth, eyelids, eyebrows, and lashes develop.

During the fifth month, the doctor can usually hear the heartbeat for the first time. He does this by placing a stethoscope against the mother's abdomen. By listening carefully he can hear the tiny thump-thump! The mother will probably begin feeling the baby move inside her now, too. That is an exciting moment!

In the sixth month, the baby will be able to open his eyes but of course, because there is no light in the uterus, he won't actually see anything.

During the seventh, eighth, and ninth months, the fetus grows very fast. He will gain more weight and begin to practice sucking. Some babies even suck their thumbs while still in the uterus. Of course, learning to suck is very important since this is how he will eat after he is born. You may be wondering how the baby is fed *before* he is born. That's another interesting story!

How is a fetus fed?

Since the baby cannot eat or drink and since he does not breathe yet, nourishment and oxygen must be supplied to him by his mother's blood. While the baby is developing within the uterus, his body is attached to the lining of the uterus by a tube called the *umbilical cord*. It connects the baby's abdomen with the mother's uterus. Just where the cord attaches to the uterus there is a flat spongy, organ called the *placenta* which is full of tiny blood vessels.

Both the baby's and the mother's blood circulate through the vessels in the placenta. However, the mother's blood never actually mixes with the baby's. Instead, the nourishment and oxygen pass through the thin walls of the mother's blood vessels into the vessels which lead to the cord. Then the umbilical cord carries the blood, with its nourishment and oxygen, into the baby's body. The cord also transports the baby's body waste materials to the placenta, where it passes from the cord vessels into those of the mother.

60 And so even though the baby doesn't eat and breathe the way you do, he does get all the food and oxygen he needs until he is born.

By the time the fetus is nine months old, his lungs are ready to begin working as soon as he is born. He also has a layer of fat under his skin to help keep him warm. The uterus has now stretched about as much as it can! Things are getting crowded in there and the fetus should be perfectly able to live outside his mother's body. Thus it is time to be born. The miracle of birth is about to happen!

How does she know?

Before we discuss the actual birth itself, you may have several other questions about pregnancy. Young people often want to know,

"How does a woman know that she is going to have a baby?"

Usually her first clue is that she will not have her menstrual period. By the time she misses a second period, she usually suspects that she might be pregnant. There are other signs. Her breasts will become larger and somewhat tender. She may feel tired and a little nauseated. At this point, she should probably visit a doctor. There, through a special kind of examination, he will be able to tell whether or not she is pregnant.

"Is a woman sick while she is pregnant?" is another question often asked. The answer is no. Pregnancy is a very natural process and women often feel especially well and happy while pregnant. They are excited that a new baby is on the way and this helps to make them feel healthy and cheerful. Of course, it's possible that while she's pregnant a woman might have some other illness like a cold or the flu. Or she may not feel well due to a special problem with her pregnancy. But this is the exception. Normally a woman can expect to feel just fine.

"Why do her breasts get larger during pregnancy?" The breasts are getting ready for their role in feeding the new baby. Glands within her breasts enlarge and are preparing to produce milk after the baby's birth. If the mother wants to, she may feed the baby by letting him suck or "nurse" on her nipples. Some mothers prefer to feed their babies with a bottle. Either method is good as long as the baby is getting enough to satisfy him.

You may wonder, "Why do women get so big while they are pregnant?" During the first few months of pregnancy, you will not even be able to tell that a woman is pregnant by looking at her. That's because the baby is still very, very tiny. However, as the baby grows, the mother's uterus will become larger and larger. By the late months of pregnancy, the uterus may hold a six or seven or even ten pound baby, plus the placenta and the bag of waters. Of course, the uterus can't stay "hidden" down inside the pelvis when it is so full and large. So it begins to push up and out within the abdomen and becomes more and more noticeable. When a woman is about to deliver her baby, she may look very large. Remember though, this is *not* fat. Rather, it is a lovely sign that she is about to have a baby.

Following nine months of pregnancy, the woman's body begins to get ready for delivery. A baby is ready to be born when it is able to live in the outside world, yet is still small enough to pass through the birth canal. If the baby is too large to pass through the vagina, a relatively simple operation called a *caeserean section* is performed. During this surgery, the woman is given an anesthetic. Then the doctor takes the baby from the uterus through an incision which he has made in the abdomen. However, in most cases, the baby will be delivered by its normal route through the vagina, and surgery is unnecessary.

As the uterus prepares to help push the baby out through the mother's body, the woman will feel the muscles beginning to work. The "squeezing" action of these muscles is called contraction. When the contractions begin, we say the woman is *in labor.* Labor is a very good word to describe the process of giving birth to a baby. Labor means work and having a baby *is* hard work. But it's a normal and satisfying kind of work.

After a woman has had contractions for a while, she will probably want to go to the hospital. There she will be met by her doctor and nurses who will help to deliver her baby. Labor may last a very short time (perhaps only one hour) or it may take longer (eight or more hours). However long or short her labor is, she will be well cared for and helped by the doctor and nurses.

Delivering a baby

Let's take a closer look at what happens during delivery. Throughout the pregnancy, the uterus has remained quiet and the opening into the uterus, the cervix, has remained almost closed. But now that the baby is ready to be born, the cervix slowly begins to stretch and the opening gets larger. At the same time, the muscles of the uterus and abdomen begin to contract and relax—contract and relax. Over a period of time, the cervix becomes large enough to allow the baby to be pushed through into the vagina. The baby is usually born head first.

The head is the largest part of a new baby. However, it is still very soft and flexible. The skull bones aren't hard and rigid. They may even overlap a bit just above the baby's forehead. Because these bones can overlap each other, the baby's head can be made smaller for that brief time while he is being born. After birth, the spot on the head where the bones overlapped will feel soft and you'll even be able to feel the baby's pulse at that place. This is sometimes called the baby's "soft spot", although the correct name is the *fontanel*. During the first few months of the baby's life, the bones in his skull will become firm and rigid enough to protect the brain inside.

Minutes after the baby has pushed itself through the cervix and into the vagina, it will be born. Having a baby is not only hard work for the mother but it is hard work for the baby too. He tells the world just how he feels about it by letting out a lusty cry right after he's born. Even though he's crying, the doctor and nurses are happy. They know that a baby's first cry is important because that shows that he is breathing properly.

Often mothers choose to remain awake during their baby's birth (though some choose to be anesthetized). It can be a very thrilling experience to watch your own baby being born. Many delivery rooms have mirrors placed so that the mother can watch the birth. A mother may be crying too, after the baby is born, but she'll be crying for joy! After waiting so long for this new baby, she is happy that her little son or daughter has finally arrived!

When the baby is born, the umbilical cord will still be connected to the placenta inside the uterus. The doctor will cut the cord and then apply a clamp to the stub of cord on the baby's abdomen. This cutting of the cord does not hurt either the mother or the baby since there are no nerves in the cord. Soon the stub of cord on the baby's abdomen will dry up and drop off, leaving the navel or belly button.

Within minutes after the baby is born and the cord cut, the placenta (sometimes called the afterbirth) will also be pushed out by the contractions of the uterus.

Following the delivery, the mother will be sent to another room in the hospital where she will rest and relax for several days. The happy father may come for visits and then will take her and the new baby home to begin their new life together.

Quiz:
1. The fetus is contained within a sac of fluid called the _____ .
2. During the first seven weeks of pregnancy a baby is called an _____ .
3. From about the third month on, the baby

is called a _____ .

4. The umbilical cord forms a connection between the baby's _____ and the mother's _____ .

True or False:

1. During the third month of pregnancy the doctor can hear the baby's heartbeat. _____

2. A baby has a brain and spinal cord by the end of the second month of pregnancy. ____

3. A mother will feel the baby moving within her during the first month. _____

4. The mother's blood mixes with the baby's blood during pregnancy. _____

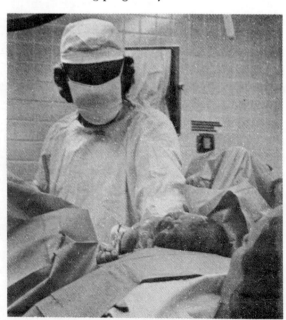

6

There are a few other things we want to talk
about before this book ends. If you have read
carefully and looked at the pictures, you have
not only learned new things, but you've also
added many new words to your vocabulary.
Any time you learn something new and exciting, you want to tell someone! You may be
tempted to share your new knowledge about
growing up with friends, only to find that
they don't know anything about it yet. Then
what do you say?

Children should first hear the story of the
meaning of sex and growing up from their
parents. There are good reasons for this. For
example, not all children are ready to hear
about menstruation at the same age. Your

parents may have explained it to you when you were nine or ten. Your eleven-year-old friend may not know yet. Rather than hearing the story from you, it would be much better if she could hear it from from her mom or dad.

Another problem with talking about sex with just anyone is that you may be told things that aren't true. Other young people may *think* they are telling you the truth when, in fact, they have the story all mixed up.

That's why it's wise to share your feelings and ask your questions about sex with your parents or some other special person who will be able to answer your questions correctly. It's natural that as time goes on, you will want to share some things with a close friend but be careful about telling "everything you know" to just anyone. Sexual matters are like money matters. Money can be talked about freely at home but you don't usually tell the neighbors or a casual friend how much the new family car cost or what Mom paid for her new dress. Information like this is usually labeled "confidential"!

You will, however, find boys and girls who think it's sophisticated or "smart" to talk about sex with everyone. They may not have the facts right or even know the right words. Still, they talk away, trying to impress others with their "secrets."

Others may use slang or dirty words when talking about sex. It's usually because they simply don't know the right words. Their ignorance shows! Of course, some kids just like to shock others by using bad language. This is a sign that they have not grown up emotionally and socially. Ephesians 5:29 tells us very plainly, "Don't use bad language. Say only what is good and helpful to those you are talking to, and what will give them a blessing."

Along with using bad language, some kids like to tell "dirty jokes". The sad thing about this is that these jokes, called "dirty", may make you think that sex is dirty. This is not true. Rather the stories become "dirty" because the person telling them is making fun of something which is really right and good.

Everyone enjoys a funny story or a good joke. But is pregnancy, or a menstrual period or sexual intercourse something to make fun of? No! They are all part of a wonderful plan which God has created. He is not pleased when we ridicule or make light of what he has made. Instead, like the psalmist David, we should be glad and thankful to God for our bodies which are so "wonderfully made".

Masturbation

Another issue which young people face is that of *masturbation*. Masturbation refers to the handling of one's genital organs until an intense sexual sensation called *orgasm* or climax is felt. In sexually mature boys, this pleasurable climax is accompanied by a discharge of semen.

Though masturbation is common among all young people, it's more frequent among boys.

For many years, young people were told that masturbating would lead to pimples, illness or even an emotional breakdown. Boys were told that if they masturbated too much, they would "use up" all their semen. Girls were told that masturbation would make them sterile (unable to have children). We know now that these things simply aren't true.

Many doctors feel that masturbation is something which takes place as a normal part of a boy or girl's growing up. However, as that young person grows and matures, we would expect him to "outgrow" his need for this kind of gratification or pleasure. It's similar to a baby sucking on a bottle or on his thumb. He likes to do it. It feels good to him. However, as he grows and matures, we expect the need for sucking to disappear.

As a young person matures and marries, the desire to masturbate will often disappear. It's probably smart not to let masturbation become a deeply set habit which may be very hard to break. Most young people want to exercise control over this practice. They don't want it to take the place of other activities or being with friends.

V.D.

In recent years, venereal disease (sometimes just called V.D.) has become an increasing problem for young people. The three more common venereal diseases are *syphilis, gonorrhea,* and *herpes.* These diseases can be very serious if left untreated. Open sores and pain may result. However, with proper medical care, they can be cured or controlled.

Syphilis, gonorrhea, and herpes are passed from person to person through sexual activity. Rarely do you get the disease any other way. For the Christian young person who follows the Bible's teaching that sexual intercourse belongs only in a marriage relationship, V.D. will not be a problem.

Homosexuality

Usually as children grow up and mature physically, they become interested in someone of the opposite sex. Teenagers date and enjoy boy-girl relationships. Later men and women marry and have sexual intercourse.

Sometimes, however, a man is sexually attracted to another man. Or, a woman is sexually attracted to another woman. These individuals usually choose not to date or marry someone of the opposite sex. Rather they choose to live in a close, sexual relationship with a person of the same sex. This is called homosexuality. People practicing homosexuality are also referred to as "gay".

The Bible tells us that God intends for men and women to be sexually attracted to each other. Homosexuality is not in his plan for us.

Someone special

As you approach your teen years (or maybe you're already a teenager) there will be times

when you may have doubts about yourself. You may think that you're not popular enough or that other people don't like you. You may worry a lot about how you look or how you sound when you talk. Girls worry about their hair and their complexion and clothes, and boys are afraid they won't make the baseball team or place in the track meet. Both boys and girls worry about each other. They wonder whether they'll be liked and be popular with the opposite sex. When you are feeling "down" and unsure of yourself, remember two things: you are a special person . . . and you are unique.

What do we mean by "special"? Simply that to certain people you are a very particular and important person. For example, when God placed you in this world, he put you into the care of two people—your parents. Those parents have taken care of you since you were an infant. They've been happy and proud of your accomplishments. They have loved you and taken an interest in every part of your life. They may *like* many other children in the world, but they *love* you as only a parent can. To them you are "special". No other child can ever take your place.

You are also special to other people like your grandparents, your aunts and uncles, your cousins, your favorite teachers, or a particular friend. You play an important part in their lives. You are "special" to them.

Some boys and girls seem to have many

friends. Others are close to just one or two people. The important thing is that we all feel special to at least a few people. If we do, (whether to parents, friends, or God) it makes us feel loved and wanted and secure.

Perhaps there's someone reading this who is thinking, "But what about me? My parents don't love me and I don't feel wanted. I'm not special to anyone!"

It's sad but true. Not all mothers and fathers love their children and take care of them as they should. Some children are even ignored and neglected. Some are physically mistreated. When this is true, it's very hard, indeed, for that young person to feel loved and wanted.

Other young people may live in homes where their parents give them everything they want—money, toys, a T.V., clothes, a nice room. Still the child feels unhappy because the parents have not given him the thing he wants most, love and attention.

If you don't feel loved and accepted, it's very important that you receive help with your problem. If at all possible, try to talk to your parents about how you feel. Find out if what you think is really true. Sometimes, parents just have a very hard time showing their love for their children, even though inside they love them very much. If, for some reason, you can't talk to your parents, go to a trusted pastor or school counselor. Tell them how you feel. Not only might they be able to help you, they may also be able to talk with your parents and help in working out this problem.

Also, be sure that you have the right attitude toward your parents. Are you kind and loving to them? Do you try to understand how they feel? Or are you sometimes ungrateful, stubborn and hard to live with? Remember, your parents are not only to love and care for you—you are to love and respect them also.

Perhaps the best news of all is that you *are* loved by God. He does not turn away anyone who comes to him through faith in Jesus Christ. Even when you feel rejected by others, God accepts and loves you, just as you are. You *are* special to him!

In addition to being a special person, you are also a very unique person. That means *you are like no one else.* There is only one person in the whole world like you—and that's you! You have particular talents and your own little hangups. Some things are very easy for you, others are hard. Maybe you play the piano well but you're not very good at sports. Or perhaps you're a real whiz at math but you can't stand English. You may be an outgoing and friendly person or perhaps you're quiet and shy. You may be tall and slender or short and not so slender!

All these things—your physical appearance, your likes and dislikes, your talents and weaknesses, your personality, your race, your environment—combine to make you a unique person. There is no one else quite like you.

You are both special and unique because God made you that way. The good news is that he loves you just like you are. In the Bible I John 3:1 says, "See how very much our heavenly Father loves us, for he allows us to be called his children—think of it—and we really are!" Even if you feel unloved by parents or other people, God really cares. You *are* important to him.

Sometimes young people have a hard time accepting and liking themselves. They worry a lot about what others think of them. But God wants you to have the proper feelings about yourself. He tells you to be humble, that is, not to be a boastful person, always bragging about yourself and demanding your right. Yet, at the same time, you are to realize that because you've been so loved by God you can feel good about yourself. You may see yourself as an important and worthwhile person, because you know that God loves and accepts you. If he loves you, you can like yourself!

With the right attitude toward yourself, other people and God, you can look forward to a life that will be happy and useful.

"And be sure of this—that I (Christ) am with you always, even to the end of the world".

GLOSSARY

Abdomen (AB-duh-men). The lower part of the body, commonly called the stomach or belly.

Acne (AK-nee). A skin condition, characterized by pimples and blackheads, common among adolescents.

Adolescence (ad-uh-LES-ens). That period of time between childhood and adulthood—usually the teen years.

Afterbirth. The placenta which is expelled after the birth of a baby.

Amniotic fluid (AM-nee-o-tic fluid). Fluid which surrounds the baby while it is still in the uterus.

Anus (A-nus). The opening through which a bowel movement passes.

"Bag of Waters". The sac within the uterus which contains the amniotic fluid and baby.

Birth Control. A deliberate act to prevent pregnancy.

Cervix (SER-vix). The opening from the vagina into the uterus.

Caesarean (se-ZAIR-ee-an). The delivery of a baby through the abdomen by an incision made in the uterus by a doctor when the woman cannot delivery normally.

Chromosome (KROH-muh-sohm). Thread-like particles found within the cell nucleus that contain genes.

Circumcision (ser-kum-SIZ-jun). The operation of cutting away the loose fold of skin from around the tip of the penis.

Clitoris (KLI-tor-is). A small pea-sized female organ located in front of the urethra.

Conception (kon-SEP-shun). The uniting of the sperm and egg.

Contraction (kon-TRAK-shun). The tightening and relaxing of the uterine muscle during labor.

Ejaculation (ee-JACK-yoo-lay-shun). The discharge of semen from the penis.

Embryo (EM-bree-oh). The fertilized egg from time of conception to 8 weeks.

Endocrine (EN-doh-crin). Glands whose secretions pass directly into the blood stream, such as the thyroid.

Erection (ee-RECK-shun). The hardening and enlarging of the penis as its spongy tissues fill with blood.

Fallopian tubes (fa-LO-pee-an tubes). Small tubes leading from the ovaries to the uterus, through which the egg passes.

Fertilization (FER-til-i-zay-shun). The joining of the egg and the sperm.

Fetus (FEE-tus). The unborn baby in the uterus *after* the first 8 weeks.

Follicle (FOL-i-cul). The tiny blister-like sac on the surface of the ovary containing the egg.

Fontanel (fon-tan-EL). The spaces between the five bony pieces which make up a baby's skull. The largest space is often called a baby's "soft spot" and is located just above the middle of a baby's forehead at the hair line.

Fraternal Twins (fra-TURN-al twins). Two babies born at the same time but may be of the opposite sex; two egg cells are fertilized by two sperm.

Gene (JEEN). The small part of the chromosome which determines inherited traits.

Genital (JEN-i-tal). Referring to the sexual or reproductive organs.

Gland. An organ of the body which produces hormones. There are six glands in the body, such as the ovaries and testes.

Glans. The rounded tip of the penis, exposed after circumcision or when the foreskin is pushed back.

Gonad (GO-nad). The ovaries in women, testicles in men: the sex glands.

Gonorrhea (gon-or-REE-a). A venereal disease.

Herpes (HER-peas). A venereal disease.

Homosexuality. A strong sexual attraction between two people of the same sex.

Hormone (HOR-mown). A chemical substance produced by a gland in the body and carried to other parts of the body through the blood stream.

Identical twins. Two babies of the same sex born at the same time; one fertilized egg grows into two babies instead of one.

Labia (LAY-bee-ah). The external folds of flesh and skin which surround the opening of the vagina.

Labor. The contracting of the muscles of the uterus which cause the cervix to open and allow the baby to be born.

Larynx (LAR-inks). The voicebox.

Masturbation (mas-tur-BAY-shun). The fondling of one's genital organs until an intense sexual sensation called orgasm or climax is felt.

Menstruation (men-stroo-AY-shun). A monthly discharge of blood and tissue from the uterus in girls.

Nocturnal emission. Wet dream: a discharge of semen from the penis while the male is sleeping; often accompanied by sexual dream.

Orgasm (OR-gazm). An intense sexual feeling felt primarily in the genital area (also called climax).

Ovum (O-vum). The female egg cell produced by the ovary.

Ovary (OH-va-ree). The two almond-shaped sex glands of the woman. They produce the egg or ovum. These glands also produce hormones which give a woman her female sexual traits.

Ovulation (oh-vyoo-LAY-shun). The release of an egg by the ovary. This usually occurs monthly.

Penis (PEE-niss). The male sex organ through which urine and semen pass out of the body.

Pituitary gland (pi-TOO-i-ter-ee gland). The "master gland" of the body located at the base of the brain.

Placenta (pla-SEN-ta). Afterbirth: The spongy organ on the wall of the uterus which provides nourishment for the fetus through the umbilical cord.

Pregnancy (PREG-nan-see). The time during which a woman is carrying an unborn baby in her uterus; from conception to birth.

Puberty (PEW-bur-tee). The period of time when a young person's sexual organs begin to function.

Sanitary napkins. Absorbent pads worn during menstruation to collect the menstrual flow.

Scrotum (SKROH-tum). The sac of skin containing the testicles.

Semen (SEE-men). The whitish fluid which contains sperm and is discharged from the penis.

Sexual intercourse (SEX-shoe-al IN-ter-cors). The act whereby the erect penis is inserted into the vagina.

Sperm. The male sex cell.

Sterile. Unable to produce children.

Syphilis (SIF-ill-is). A venereal disease.

Tampon (TAM-pon). An absorbent roll of cotton inserted into the vagina to collect the menstrual flow.

Testicles (TESS-ti-kals). The two male sex glands contained in the scrotum, which produce sperm.

Umbilical cord (um-BILL-i-cal cord). The cord connecting the unborn baby with the placenta; contains blood vessels.

Urethra (yoo-REE-thra). The tube from the urinary bladder through which urine flows.

Uterus (YOO-ter-us). The muscular organ in a woman which contains the unborn baby. In a female not pregnant, the menstrual flow comes from the uterus.

Vagina (va-JY-na). The passageway which leads from the uterus to the outside of a woman's body.

Venereal disease (ve-NEE-ree-al disease). An infection like syphilis or gonorrhea which mainly affects the sexual organs and is usually spread through sexual intercourse.

Wet dream. (See nocturnal emission)

Answers to Quizzes

p. 15
3. orifice
8. anus
4. abdomen
6. urethra
5. vagina
2. fallopian tubes
1. labia
7. ovaries

p. 21
1. testicles
2. erection
3. semen
4. scrotum
5. urethra

p. 27
1. false
2. true
3. false
4. true
5. false

p. 28
1. true
2. false
3. true
4. false
5. true

p. 42
1. ovary
2. ovulation
3. through the Fallopian tube
4. about once a month
5. menstruation
6. 3-6 days

p. 46
1. ejaculation
2. nocturnal emission
3. 12-14

p. 55
1. conception or fertilization
2. intercourse
3. 5-7 days
4. 9 months
5. 23
6. genes
7. girl
8. fraternal
9. same

p. 65
1. "bag of waters"
2. embryo
3. fetus
4. navel and the mother's uterus

p. 66
1. false
2. true
3. false
4. false

89175